Grab

by Jacob Blakeslee
illustrated by Chris Vallo

Practice Decodable 20

Mc Graw Hill Education

Bothell, WA • Chicago, IL • Columbus, OH • New York, NY

MHEonline.com

Send all inquiries to:
McGraw-Hill Education
8787 Orion Place
Columbus, OH 43240

ISBN: 978-0-02-144974-3
MHID: 0-02-144974-0

Printed in China.

8 9 10 11 12 DSS 27 26 25 24 23

Grab a bat.
Then get a hit.

Grab a mat.

And take a nap.

Grab a dog.
Grab a cap.
Then run and run.

Grab big cans.
And drum and drum.

Grab a top.
Then make it spin.

Grab a mom.

And get a hug.